MAR

THE COMPLETE GARDENER

PLANTING
& GROWING

Ballantine Books

Ballantine Books
A division of Random House of Canada Limited
1265 Aerowood Drive
Mississauga, ON L4W 1B9

INFACT Publishing Ltd.
66 Portland St., 2nd Floor
Toronto, ON M5V 2M8

CTV Television Network Ltd.
250 Yonge St., 18th Floor
Toronto, ON M5B 2N8

Canadian Cataloguing in Publication Data

Cullen, Mark, 1956—
      Planting & growing
(Mark Cullen's Complete gardener series)
Accompanied by video.
Includes index.
ISBN 0-345-39831-9

1. Planting (Plant culture). 2. Gardening. I. Title. II.
Title: Planting and growing. III. Series: Cullen, Mark,
1956— . Mark Cullen's Complete gardener series.

SB473.C85 1996   635'.04   C96-930029-8

PHOTOS: Janet Davis—p. 16, 26, 58, 62; Ted Johnston—p. 46
SENIOR EDITOR: Wendy Thomas
HORTICULTURAL EDITOR: Denis Flanagan
COPY EDITOR: Sylvia Gilchrist
CTV CO-ORDINATOR: Glen Dickout, Manager, Special Projects
PROJECT MANAGER: Susan Yates, INFACT Publishing
COVER AND TEXT DESIGN AND ILLUSTRATION ART: ArtPlus:
    Brant Cowie, Dave Murphy and Jerry Stapley
SPECIAL THANKS: Dan Matheson, Canada am; Jean and John
    Farintosh; Aunt Charlotte and Uncle Tom; Len Cullen,
    my Dad; and especially, Mary for her help and support.

M+M Communications, Unionville, ON is the publishing imprint of Mary and Mark Cullen.

Printed and bound in Canada by Metropole Litho Inc.

TABLE OF CONTENTS

INTRODUCTION

"What exactly do you do?" I am sometimes asked, in reference to my "day job." My response to that is to suggest that my professional goal in life is to remove the hocus-pocus, or the barriers, that Canadians imagine stand between them and success in the garden.

This book and video are a natural extension of what I do with great passion every day. My intent is to show you how to get the most out of your garden and to do it by minimizing the "work" (maintenance) and maximizing what I believe to be the most pleasurable aspects of gardening, including lounging around the yard in a favourite chair or hammock.

My good friend Dan Matheson is no gardening dummy. Truth is, he is a fast learner with more enthusiasm than most of us can imagine. He also has a habit of asking the very questions that Canadian gardeners (and non gardeners!) have on their minds at the time. I think you will enjoy this book and video as we simplify gardening and help you to get the most from your Canadian garden through *The Complete Gardener.*

In this volume, I'll introduce you to the fundamentals of good growing practices, starting from the ground up! With the information in this book, you'll understand how plants function and the part that good soil and adequate heat, light, and water play in the development of healthy, beautiful, and productive plants.

MARK CULLEN

SOIL

. . . .

I was taught by a gardener years ago to respect the "word" — you keep *soil*, but throw away *dirt*.

The most fundamental role of soil in the garden is to provide a medium in which the roots of plants can anchor themselves. Soil also acts like a food cupboard, holding moisture and nutrients that the plant takes in through its roots.

Soil is a thriving colony of living micro-organisms with each micro-organism dependent on the other and each helping to decompose organic materials that are found in and on the soil. As these organic materials are broken down by the micro-organisms, the nutritious by-products released through the process improve the soil's texture and health. This wonderful symbiotic relationship produces the best soil — a plant's growth, and the growth of other organisms, is supported by the soil; the plant dies, it decays and renourishes the soil from which it came. Beginning today, think of soil as a medium teaming with life. Once you think of and understand soil in this way, you are on your way to gardening success.

THE COMPOSITION OF SOIL

I know the temptation we all have of rushing home with a new plant and wanting to put it in the ground immediately. However, before you dig that hole, your plant will thank you if you understand something about soil. Let us look at types of soil and how soil can be improved.

Soil is made of
- small particles of rocks and minerals
- dead and decaying organic matter
- water and air
- plant and animal organisms

When these components are in balance, you have healthy soil that is a host to earthworms and supports many types of growth. The challenge to the gardener is to create and maintain this balance and to achieve *friable* soil — soil that is crumbly, is easily worked, and contains just the right amount of moisture.

MINERALS

The effects of weather — wind, water, freezing, thawing — over many eons have broken large boulders and rocks into minute particles. These particles provide minerals, such as iron, calcium, magnesium, potassium, iron, phosphorus, and boron, which are necessary to good growing. I'll talk more about minerals in Chapter 2.

The size of the mineral particles helps us categorize soil into types: sand, clay, silt, and loam.

Sandy soil particles are larger than other particles. This type of soil has a lot of air between the particles, making it loose and light. When you

Composition of sandy soil

deep and porous topsoil

very few stones

perfect drainage

sandstone rock

pick it up, it falls a part easily. Sandy soil

- is quick to warm up in the spring;
- is easy to dig and work with;
- drains quickly so nutrients are not held in it for long;
- needs frequent watering for plants to survive;
- is easily picked up by strong winds and blown about.

Clay soil particles are much smaller than sand particles and because they are so small, air has difficulty getting between them. The particles nestle close together, forming a soil that is heavy, compact, and very moisture-retentive. Clay soil

- holds nutrients and moisture well (this quality makes it worth improving this type of soil);

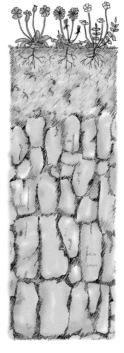

Composition of clay soil

compact heavy topsoil

blocky subsoil with cracks that fill up with water

poor drainage

- takes longer to warm up in the spring;
- forms a hard crust on its surface in hot dry weather;
- can be heavy to dig.

Silt soil particles are larger than clay and smaller than sand particles. They make a slow-draining soil that is rather powdery when dry.

Loam soil contains a balance of sand, clay, and silt. This mixture forms a soil that does not drain too quickly, but drains quickly enough that roots are not robbed of oxygen. A loam soil holds nutrients and this results in plants being continuously supplied with food.

ORGANIC MATTER

One of the most important components of a loamy soil is organic matter. Examples of organic matter are manure, leaf mould, peat moss, grass clippings, kitchen wastes, and sawdust. A word of warning, though: organic matter should be partly or wholly decomposed before it is added to soil. I'll be telling you more about this later when I get to one of my favourite topics, composting!

Whether your soil is sand, clay, silt, or loam adding organic material will improve it. Sandy soil will retain water and nutrients longer and clay soil will drain more quickly with the addition of partially or well-rotted compost or other organic matter.

Water and Air

As you begin to understand more about soil, you will also become aware of how important the plants' roots are. Not only do they transport water and nutrients to the plant but they also breathe. Soil full of water has no room for air. Roots when deprived of oxygen, drown. Your aim is to keep the soil *balanced* so that it drains well but does not dry too quickly.

Plant and Animal Organisms

As your soil improves with the addition of organic material, subterranean creatures — microscopic as well as visible — will come to feast, leaving behind their own valuable additions. These good bugs help to break down materials in the soil that improve the soil's structure.

Earthworms are a sign of healthy soil. How can you attract earthworms to your garden? Good old organic matter — compost! Dig it in or pile it on top of beds as a mulch. The worms will eat their way through this material, leaving behind castings that contain more minerals than the soil which they have digested. I am glad fishing is not included in my list of hobbies as I would have to compost twice as much to take care of both bait and botany!

There is more good news about earthworms. They can burrow as deep as 1.8 m (6 feet) and as they burrow, they aerate the soil, allowing water and air to penetrate. Their travels also help to mix the soil up, stirring it, in effect, to bring valuable nutrients closer to the surface for use by the plants.

Micro-organisms such as bacteria, fungi, and yeasts play their part in helping plant and animal matter break down, releasing their nutrients into the soil. Most micro-organisms need warmth, moisture, and air in order to do their work.

All these plant and animal organisms, both large and small, are important in the composting process.

COMPOSTING

I have a passion for composting. Composting is one of my favourite garden activities — although it is Mother Nature and not me who is doing the real work! Unlike me, Dan Matheson, my gardening buddy from Canada am, is not a career gardener but, with little effort, he is able to enjoy the results he obtains from his composter.

Composting makes me feel good because I'm recycling garden and kitchen wastes instead of sending them to landfill sites. It also makes my garden feel good when I dig in the crumbly dark material called *humus* which results from composting. Not only is well-rotted compost full of nutrients, but it also improves the *tilth* — the physical condition —

of the soil. Improving your soil is part of gardening and adding composted materials to your garden gives back to the soil nutrients that have been taken from it by the growing plants.

Composting is a process that occurs naturally in forests and uncultivated fields. Leaves fall from trees, tall grasses crumple to the ground, animals and micro-organisms die. The remains of these plants and animals are acted on by bacteria that aid in their decomposition. As the remains decompose, they are incorporated in the soil by the actions of earthworms, insects, and small animals. In this natural state, composting is a slow process, but this is one of the ways Mother Nature, over millions of years, has provided us with the thin layer of valuable topsoil that covers our planet to varying depths. However, we can produce compost more quickly, often in one gardening season, by providing the correct conditions for insects and micro-organisms to do their work.

Get the kids involved in composting — although the chances are pretty good that it was they who got you involved! Composting is a great way to introduce children to the most basic gardening fundamental — the source of all life in the garden.

Poor Tilth
Lumps of soil are difficult to break up.

Good Tilth
Soil is crumbly and easy to work.

Compost is the nurturing environment for all roots, and composting is the best place for kids to begin to learn an appreciation for what goes on in the garden.

CONDITIONS FOR COMPOSTING

The conditions that bacteria need to work best in soil are the same conditions that they need to work in a compost pile: a balance of warmth, moisture, and air.

WARMTH: In the winter, the composting process virtually stops, but the cycle of freezing and thawing that takes place in most winters helps to break down the cells in the material, making it ready for the action of the bacteria in the warmer weather. In milder parts of the country, decomposition may continue during the winter but at a very slow rate. As the weather warms up in the spring, the bacteria become active and as they start their work, they generate their own heat. Temperatures of up to 70°C (160°F) are often reached in composts. At such high temperatures, many weed seeds, insect eggs and larvae are destroyed.

MOISTURE: Moisture is another requirement to keep decomposition going. Some of the materials you put in the composter will already contain moisture — things such as tea bags, fruit and vegetable peelings, and freshly cut grass — but if your composter is full of materials such as straw or dead leaves, you may have to sprinkle in some water to provide the bacteria with the environment they like best. *The contents of the pile should have the consistency of a wrung-out sponge.* If you squeeze the composting

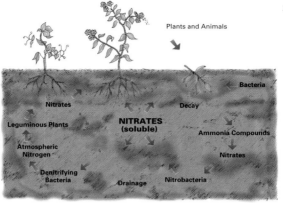

The Nitrogen Cycle. Nitrogen from the atmosphere reaches the soil and plants. When plants decay, the nitrogen is processed and released for use by living plants.

materials, no water should run out. If the materials just crumble, the pile is too dry. I guess you will be considered an active gardener when your neighbours watch you hand squeeze to test your compost. It's easier to maintain the moisture balance if your composter is covered, even if it's only a well-anchored plastic sheet covering your pile.

AIR: The final condition for good composting is the provision of air. Incorporating air into your compost pile will prevent the contents from becoming smelly. Good compost has a slightly earthy smell, but if yours starts to give off a bad smell, the problem is easy to fix. Simply turning the pile over adds air. You can use a fork or an aerating tool to turn the pile. You can buy either one specially made for the purpose or use a stick, pole, or shovel to plunge into the centre of the pile to stir things up. After stirring, add 2.5 cm to 5 cm (1 to 2 inches) of garden soil. Another option is to build the pile around a ventilating stack. Commercial air stacks can be purchased at garden centres, but you can also make your own from a perforated pipe or wire mesh formed into a cylinder. Ventilating stacks provide enough oxygen to the centre of the pile that you don't have to turn the compost.

TYPE OF COMPOSTER

I was tempted to call this section "To bin or not to bin!" In other words, is a bin necessary? If you use a bin, what kind should you choose?

First, let's look at the pile versus container question.

COMPOST PILE: A pile can be every bit as good at composting as the fanciest, most expensive commercial composter. However, it will work best and produce more quickly under certain conditions. Space can be one of these considerations. To a certain degree, the larger a pile, the better it will work. Even if your garden area is small, you can still build an open pile. You will just have to wait longer for the results. An open pile should also be covered in some fashion to maintain a good moisture balance. Open piles can be easier to turn, as long as they are not extremely high or wide. A disadvantage to an open pile is the possibility that the kitchen wastes can attract rodents. If you absolutely must have an open pile, bury kitchen scraps deep in the middle.

BINS: Bins have many advantages: they hold the organic matter above the ground where air can circulate through it, they're easier to keep out of sight in a garden, they usually come with covers, and they are more likely to be rodent-proof — though a determined mouse can get in just about any bin. Depending on the design and materials used in construction, bins also may offer more insulation, thereby extending your composting season.

If you decide on a bin, you still have a further choice to make: home-made or purchased? Let's look at homemade bins first.

Homemade Bins. A bin can be made from objects either found about your property or easily bought: discarded skids, wire fencing, snow fencing, concrete blocks, bales of straw, wooden barrels, metal drums, garbage cans, or even garbage bags — in short, anything that can be fashioned into an enclosure can make a composting bin. It can be circular or square. with maximum dimensions of 1.5 m (5 feet) square and minimum of 90 cm (4 feet) square. Here are a few pointers to keep in mind if you're constructing your own bin:

❀ ....

Provide some kind of covering to keep snow and rain out and to discourage animals.

Compost bins showing methods of aeration. Left, a bin with holes; right, a bin with a ventilation stack.

❊ Don't build the bin too tall or you will have difficulty turning the materials.

❊ Consider constructing a door at the bottom through which you can extract finished compost.

❊ Drill 5 cm (2-inch) holes about a hand span apart to allow air to circulate if your bin is made of a garbage can or metal drum. If the bin is constructed of concrete blocks, put some of them on their sides to allow air to enter. An alternative is to use a ventilating stack as I described earlier.

Purchased Bins. Commercial bins come in many sizes, materials, shapes, and price ranges. Some are made of wood, some of recycled plastic, others of metal mesh. Fortunately, they all do the same thing: turn organic material into humus. Many bins are quite unobtrusive looking and will not be an eyesore.

A commercial bin should have all the features of a homemade bin. To help you make your decision, visit garden centres, talk to neighbours, visit the

The cost of this type of compost bin is often subsidized by towns, cities or municipalities to make composting affordable and easy for residents.

composting sites some municipalities have installed, measure your garden, decide where you want to situate the bin — then, before you make your final decision, check with your municipality to see if they sell bins to residents at a reduced price.

SITING THE COMPOST PILE

On many urban lots, you're not going to have a lot of choice about where to put the composter. Space is often at a premium and you want to keep the sunniest, most visible spots free for relaxing in and gardening. Even though compost doesn't smell, you don't really want a composter at your elbow as you sip your iced tea! If you do have some flexibility about where the composter is sited, here are a few guidelines about the ideal situation for a compost bin.

❀ The area should be protected from strong winds.

❀ The ground should be fairly level and drain well.

❀ It should be easy to get to the composter, summer and winter.

❀ A sunny spot helps commercial composters work better and faster.

❀ Wire or wooden bins are best located in a shady spot to reduce drying out.

❀ Don't put the composter directly under an eavestrough downspout as you could end up with too much water in the compost.

MATERIALS FOR COMPOSTING

Even if you garden in a small urban lot, you can find lots of materials to feed your composter. Below are two lists showing what can and can't go into your composter.

Suitable for Composting

- blood meal
- bone meal
- coffee grounds
- corn cobs and stalks (chop into small pieces)
- dead stalks and leaves from the garden
- eggshells, crushed
- flower stalks and leaves at the end of the season
- fruit peels
- grass clippings
- hay
- leaves
- lint from clothes dryer
- manure (but not pet feces)
- newspaper, black ink section only, shredded
- nut shells
- peat moss
- pine needles
- potting soil from containers and window boxes
- sawdust
- seaweed
- tea leaves
- vegetable peelings
- weeds (before seeds have set)
- wood ash
- wood chips

Not Suitable for Composting

- bones
- cat litter or pet feces
- charcoal and barbecue briquettes
- coal ashes
- diseased plants
- fatty or oily foods
- fish and meat
- plant material that has been sprayed recently with any chemical

FEEDING THE COMPOSTER

Now that you have your composter and know what can and can't go in it, you're ready to start composting.

❀
Any time is the right time to start composting — although it's true that it is a bit harder in winter! Fall and spring are the two seasons where there is more garden waste available to start filling the composter.

❀
Start with a bottom layer of finished compost, well-rotted manure, or soil, and the composting process will start more quickly as you add your materials.

❀
Composters work best when the materials are added in layers of brown and green, or according to the amount of carbon and nitrogen they contain. All organic material contains both carbon and nitrogen, but some plants have more of one than the other. For speedy composting, the carbon content should be about 20 to 1 of nitrogen. Brown materials, which are high in carbon, are such things as dried grass clippings, wood chips, sawdust, and

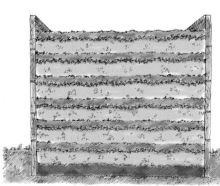

Composters work best when the materials are added in layers of brown (carbon-containing) and green (nitrogen-containing).

dead leaves. Green materials, which are high in nitrogen, are vegetable and fruit peelings, freshly cut grass, feathers, and hair. It's impossible to ensure that your compost contains the ideal ratios, but knowing that the two elements work together helps you to understand the composting process.

❀ Layer about 7.5 cm to 12.5 cm (3 to 5 inches) of carbon material alternately with 5 cm to 7.5 cm (2 to 3 inches) of nitrogen material.

❀ Add a 2.5 cm (1 inch) layer of soil approximately every 30 cm (1 foot) to introduce active microbes and cut down on fungus gnats.

❀ If the materials seem dry, sprinkle some water on the layers. A strong ammonia smell indicates the material is too wet and needs air. Alternating layers of wet and dry material will help to keep the pile evenly moist.

❀ Materials that have been chopped or shredded will break down more quickly.

SPEEDING UP THE COMPOSTING PROCESS

As I indicated above, materials that are chopped into pieces, ideally 2.5 cm (1 inch) long, will break down more quickly. By chopping or shredding, you give the bacteria more surface area to work on. There are some other tricks to get the compost cooking more quickly.

❀ Adding manure or blood meal to materials in the composter will not only add nitrogen to the mix, but will help speed up decomposition. Chicken manure is especially high in nitrogen. However, fresh manure will be too hot and could kill some bacteria so be sure any manure you use is well-rotted before adding it to your compost pile.

✿ ....

A manure tea, made in the same manner as the compost tea described below, will give the compost a kick start.

✿ ....

Commercial chemical activators contain microbes and enzymes which speed up activity and get the bacteria in a new pile working quickly.

✿ ....

Soil or finished compost will also add micro-organisms that will soon get to work on the materials in the composter.

COMPOST TEA

Use compost tea to water plants that normally wouldn't receive a helping of compost. Plants in containers, window boxes, and hanging baskets will love it.

Just mix equal parts of compost and water in a bucket or watering can. Give it a stir every few days. Then allow the compost to settle to the bottom of the bucket and the tea will be ready to use. The same compost can be used to make several batches of tea. When you've made all the brews you want, put the remaining compost back in the pile or spread it over a bed. Make manure tea in the same way, replacing the compost with well-rotted manure.

COMPOSTING PROBLEMS

Composting does take time to produce what I like to call "black gold" (compost is that valuable in the garden); but, what if your compost seems to be taking forever? Or, what if it's turned into a smelly, slimy mess? Fortunately, composting problems are easy to fix.

❋

Problem: Compost has decomposed into a runny, bad-smelling horror.

Possible causes: Materials may have been cut or shredded into pieces that are too small. Anything as fine as sawdust, for example, will compact more easily, leaving little space for air. Large piles, higher or wider than 1.5 m (5 feet) can become smelly because the centre has become compacted.

Solution: Add some drier and lighter materials such as straw or shredded newspaper. Break up large piles into smaller ones or add a ventilator tube. Sprinkling lime on the heap will help, but will also deplete the compost of some its nitrogen.

Prevention: Don't chop or shred materials too finely. Alternate layers of different materials. Thick layers of leaves can mat, again cutting out the air. When adding large quantities of fresh grass clippings, make the layers quite thin or mix the clippings with chunkier materials to prevent the grass from matting. Turn the pile every few weeks if smells are a problem.

❋

Problem: Nothing at all seems to be happening.

Possible causes: It can take as long as a year, or even two, for some materials to decompose.

This is more likely to happen if your pile is made up of only one type of material, such as leaves. The size of pile, especially one not made in a bin, can affect decomposition rates. A small pile will eventually decompose but will not build up the same amount of heat as a larger one. It's also possible that the materials are too dry, the pieces are too large, or the pile is being turned too frequently (more often than once a week).

Solution: Add manure, blood meal, or a commercial compost activator. Chop up pieces that are larger than 5 cm (2 inches).

Prevention: Make layers of different types of materials, aiming for balances of browns and greens. Alternate wet and dry materials. Add water if the materials seem too dry. Don't turn the pile — if you want to be sure air is getting in, just fluff the pile lightly or thrust a stick or broom handle into its centre and wiggle it a bit.

How Not to Build a Compost Pile
An indiscriminate pile of materials, completely exposed to the elements, will not decompose properly and is unsightly.

❁

Problem: Animals are attracted to the pile.

Possible causes: You might have been adding the wrong kinds of materials (refer to the list I gave you earlier). The food materials you've been adding are not decomposing quickly enough.

Solution: Bury food scraps in the centre of the pile or cover them with a good layer of soil or finished compost. Chop them into 2.5 cm (1 inch) lengths so they decompose quickly.

Prevention: Do not put meat, fish, or anything that's greasy into the composter. Consider pest-proofing your bin by using hardware cloth to close off all entry points. You will have to extend the cloth below ground level to be sure that you have a good barrier. If possible, put a latch on the lid to thwart raccoons and squirrels. Do not use poison to repel pests.

❁

Problem: Insects are swarming in and around the pile.

Possible causes: There could be too much moisture in the pile and food scraps may not be covered well.

Solution: Cover all food scraps with a layer of soil or bury them deep in the centre.

Prevention: I don't get too worried about insects in my composter — sow bugs, earwigs, and even slugs have a part to play in the composting process. Just like the micro-organisms busy at work, the bugs and insects are doing their bit. Besides, I'd rather have earwigs and slugs hard at work in my composter than chewing my lettuce or pansies in the garden!

Prevention: If you're really concerned about flies, cover food scraps with about 5 cm (2 inches) of soil.

ALKALINE AND ACID SOIL

Most plants are wonderfully tolerant of the soil they grow in, but to have the healthiest and most productive plants possible and to make life easier for you, choose plants that will thrive in your conditions. One of the conditions that can affect your garden's success and productivity is the soil's degree of acidity or alkalinity which is measured on a pH (potential of hydrogen) scale. The pH scale runs from 0 to 14, with 7 being neutral. Extremely acid soil is 4, extremely alkaline soil is 8.

IMPORTANCE OF KNOWING pH

Knowing your soil's exact pH measure is less important than knowing whether your soil tends to be acid or alkaline. Soil at the extremes of the pH scale bind minerals in the soil so that they are not available to plants. Very acidic soils are usually lacking quantities of potassium, calcium, and magnesium. Even though iron is present in alkaline soils, it is not easily released. If your plants aren't responding to your loving care, it could be that the soil is too acid or too alkaline for them.

Although most plants are happiest in the midrange, about 6 to 7, some plants prefer acid soil and others prefer alkaline soil. Sweet peas, baby's breath, lilacs, and peonies prefer alkaline, or limey,

Sweet pea is one plant that prefers an alkaline soil.

soil. Rhododendrons, azaleas, and heathers will sulk in alkaline soil — they do best in acid soil. Woodland plants are more likely to thrive if they're grown in conditions similar to those found in the wild, and that means slightly acidic soil. If you don't want to try to alter the pH of your soil, get to know the plants that will do best in the soil you have. Talk to neighbours, visit nearby parks, and get to know the staff at a local garden centre to see what other gardeners are growing successfully.

HOW TO RECOGNIZE ACID OR ALKALINE SOIL

You can't identify a soil's pH just by looking at it, but you can find some clues in your surroundings.

❋ What kinds of rock abound in your area? Limestone is a sure sign you live in an area with neutral to slightly alkaline soil. Granite indicates that the soil could be acid.

❋ Areas with low rainfall are often alkaline.

❋ An abundance of blueberries, ferns, and hemlocks is a sign of acid soil.

❋ Acid soils will often have moss on their surface, exhibit poor plant growth, and bear weeds such as plantain and dock.

One easy way to test for highly alkaline soil is to mix a spoonful of dry soil with an equal amount of white vinegar in a cup or small bottle. Shake and hold the container close to your ear. If you hear a strong fizzing noise, your soil is very alkaline. However, to be absolutely certain of your soil's pH you can buy a soil testing kit or send a sample of your soil to your provincial department of agriculture or a private testing lab.

HOW TO CHANGE THE pH

If you have soil at either end of the pH scale, my advice would be to relax and take advantage of it. Your soil is alkaline? Revel in the delights of clematis, which prefer soil on the alkaline side, and forget about rhododendrons.

Having said that, I know it's human nature to want what we can't have! So here are a few tips for altering your soil's pH.

❋ Adding ground limestone or dolomite will make acid soil more alkaline. You'll need to add more limestone to acidic heavy clay than to acidic sandy soil, though, so check the instructions on the bag carefully.

❋

Ground sulphur will make alkaline soil more acidic. Again, clay soils will need heavier treatment than sandy soils.

❋

Digging peat moss into soil will increase the acidity. It works gradually but also has the advantage of improving the texture of the soil.

❋

Compost dug into any type of soil will bring it closer to neutral.

❋

Organic matter that makes soil more acid includes sawdust, composted oak leaves, wood chips, leaf mould, and peat moss.

❋

Organic matter that makes soil more alkaline includes wood ashes, bone meal, crushed marble, crushed oyster shells.

If you are absolutely determined to grow a plant or group of plants that isn't suitable for your soil, there is some hope. Choose an appropriate part of the garden and build a raised bed with wood or stone. Dig the soil out of the new bed (add it to the compost if you have nowhere else to put it) to a depth of at least 30 cm (1 foot) below the original soil level. Fill up the new bed with triple mix (available in bags at garden centres or delivered loose in large quantities). Once you've got the new plants installed, topdress them with a mulch that satisfies their pH needs. Mulch acid-loving plants with 10 cm to 12.5 cm (4 to 5 inches) of pine needles and alkaline-loving plants with cocoa bean hulls.

Now that we've examined the components of soil and how to make compost, in the next chapter, I'll

HOW TO CREATE A RAISED BED

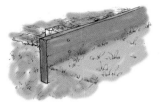

Wooden planks

Railroad ties

Short logs or poles

Stones or broken concrete

Raised beds are a solution to ground soil which is overly acidic or overly alkaline.

show you what to do with the compost you've made and other ways of making your soil more productive. We will also look more closely at the minerals in the soil and I'll explain how to replenish them.

FERTILIZING AND CONDITIONING THE SOIL

· ·

N ow that you know what a healthy garden is built on — good soil — we'll look at some ways of keeping it that way. Although the most accurate way of knowing the balance of minerals in your soil is to have it tested, the condition of your plants can give you some clues about deficiencies. If you add lots of organic matter, your soil is likely to be healthy, nutritious, and well balanced. There are times, though, when extra help is needed. Options for garden "First Aid" usually fall into two groups: organic or chemical. Before I discuss the advantages and disadvantages of each, let's look a bit more closely at the nutrients found in soil.

MORE ABOUT NUTRIENTS

Nutrients are present in varying degrees in most soils. As I said in Chapter 1, the pH level of your soil can affect how successfully nutrients are released. Here are the important nutrients and what they do.

CALCIUM
The role of calcium is to build strong cells. Calcium is present in gypsum, lime, wood ashes, bone meal, and clam and oyster shells.

MAGNESIUM
Magnesium, which is part of chlorophyll, makes plants green. Too much magnesium in soil can cause a deficiency of potassium (see below). Magnesium is found in magnesium sulphate, dolomitic limestone, and liquid seaweed.

MICRONUTRIENTS
Micronutrients are often referred to as trace elements — they are needed only in very small amounts. A gardener seldom needs to worry about them. The trace elements of boron, chlorine, cobalt, copper, iron, manganese, molybdenum, nickel, and zinc can be found in liquid seaweed.

NITROGEN (N)
Nitrogen makes stems and leaves grow and provides a deep green colour. An abundance of nitrogen can cause a plant to put its energy into green growth at the expense of flower or fruits. It also nourishes micro-organisms as they aid in decomposition. Nitrogen is present in manure, sewage sludge, blood meal, and fish emulsion. In the three-number analysis found on every fertilizer package, nitrogen is always the first, as explained in more detail following.

PHOSPHORUS (P)

Phosphorus encourages root growth, flowering, fruiting, and resistance to disease and winter damage. Rock phosphate and bone meal contain phosphorus but must be worked into the soil to be effective. Phosphorous is represented by the second number in the three-number fertilizer analysis.

POTASSIUM (K)

Potassium (also called potash) promotes strong root growth, disease resistance, and general vigour. It is usually found as part of commercial fertilizers along with nitrogen and phosphorus. Potassium is represented by the third number in the three-number analysis.

SULPHUR

Sulphur helps lower the pH in alkaline soil, encouraging acidity in soil.

FERTILIZERS

Most of the nutrients I've listed above are used in such small amounts by plants that replacing them is not necessary, especially if you use compost as a soil amendment. But nitrogen, phosphorus, and

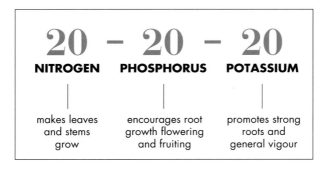

20 – 20 – 20

NITROGEN	PHOSPHORUS	POTASSIUM
makes leaves and stems grow	encourages root growth flowering and fruiting	promotes strong roots and general vigour

potassium (referred to as NPK) are used in larger amounts by plants and are used quickly.

The proportions of nitrogen, phosphorus, and potassium are indicated on the front of a bag of fertilizer by a series of three numbers. As mentioned above, in the three-number analysis nitrogen is shown first, followed by phosphorous, and then potassium. If the numbers are 20-20-20, that means that 20% of the fertilizer is nitrogen, 20% of the fertilizer is phosphorus, and 20% is potassium. You'll note that adds up to only 60%. The remaining 40% is filler or buffer. The filler is necessary because if you apply 100% of these nutrients to the soil formula, it would be too strong for the plants and cause more problems than you are trying to solve.

Knowing what these numbers represent and what each nutrient does will aid you in making an informed choice when purchasing and applying fertilizer. A high first number, for example, indicates that this fertilizer has more nitrogen than phosphorus or potassium. A 10-6-4 fertilizer would improve the green colour of your plants and improve the growth of stems and leaves. To a lesser extent, root growth and disease resistance would be strengthened. Let me caution you, however, that if your plants are already healthy and producing well, doses of fertilizer will not make them even better. Over-fertilizing, especially with chemical fertilizers, can cause excessive growth at the expense of flowering and fruiting and can burn roots.

ORGANIC VERSUS CHEMICAL FERTILIZERS

An organic fertilizer is one that is derived from animals, plants, or minerals and although they may be processed to dry them or chop them up, they are not processed chemically or mixed with synthetic materials. Examples are bone meal, blood meal, and fish emulsion. Chemical, or synthetic, fertilizers are those made from raw materials that are changed by a chemical reaction to make them able to be used by plants. Examples of chemical fertilizers are urea and superphosphate.

The advantages of organic fertilizers are:
- The nutrients are released slowly into the soil so there is less fear of overdosing the plants or burning them.
- They often contain trace elements that are good for the soil and plants.
- Some contain organic material.

The disadvantages of organic fertilizers are:
- It can take longer to see the results of the application.
- Some release their nutrients only when the soil is fairly warm.
- The nutrients are not always balanced in organic fertilizers, such as manure and compost, so they may not be suitable for the problem you are treating.

The advantages of chemical fertilizers are:
- They are released quickly into the soil, which is especially important in areas with short growing seasons.
- Low soil temperatures in cool climates or areas with short growing seasons only slightly decrease the availability of chemical fertilizers.
- It's easy to control how much you use.
- They contain no diseases or weed seeds.

The disadvantages of chemical fertilizers are:
- They don't add organic matter to the soil.
- They can kill earthworms.
- Care must be taken in their application and especially not to overdose plants; plants can become weak when chemical fertilizers are not used properly.

LIQUID FERTILIZERS

Fertilizers are available in dry or granular form or as liquids. When liquid fertilizer is applied to the plant's leaves, it's called a foliar fertilizer. If the plant you are treating has a weak root system, a foliar application of fertilizer will be less stressful. Check the product to be sure it's suitable for foliar treatment.

SHOPPING FOR FERTILIZERS

You now have an understanding about the all-important numbers on fertilizer containers. If chemical fertilizers are the solution to your gardening problem, consult with a professional at the garden centre. He or she will be able to advise you as you choose from the many products available. Buying organic fertilizers can be somewhat less complicated, but it might be hard to find them in all garden centres. Here is a list of some organic fertilizers that are usually easy to find.
- Bone meal, blood meal, fish meal, canola seed meal, and manure provide nitrogen.
- Bone meal, blood meal, fish meal, and rock phosphate provide phosphorus.
- Liquid and chopped seaweed, wood ashes, kelp meal, manure, green sand, and granite dust provide potassium.

APPLYING FERTILIZER

Fertilizer is best applied when you're preparing a new bed or when you're planting in the spring. If you are preparing a bed in the fall to be planted in the spring, use a slow-release fertilizer. A dry or granular fertilizer is easy to dig in. Unless you know the mineral content of your soil and its deficiencies, it is best to apply an organic fertilizer to prevent over-fertilizing.

For existing beds, scratch dry fertilizer into the soil around the plant. Take care not to let the fertilizer touch the plant in case it burns the parts it touches. Foliar fertilizer is often the best in these situations.

Always water after using a dry fertilizer in order to make it accessible to the plant. But, don't fertilize a wilting or sickly plant. Truth is, a plant under stress cannot benefit from fertilizer. Give it water and protection from strong sun until it seems to be restored to health. Fertilizing keeps plants healthy — it doesn't cure unhealthy ones.

RULE OF THUMB:

It is better to under-fertilize your plants than to over-fertilize. There is often a tendency to over-fertilize — if your doctor told you to take two tablets a day, would you take four?

WHEN TO FERTILIZE

In the spring:
- Dig dry fertilizer into the soil of new beds or holes before planting. Dampen seed beds

Fertilizing
When fertilizing plants ensure the fertilizer does not touch the stem or leaves. Fertilizer can be placed around the plant or in rows beside plants

with liquid starter solutions, such as transplanter 5-15-5, before sowing.

- Give lawns a high-nitrogen fertilizer very early in the spring.
- Fertilize flowers and vegetables before flowering with high phosphorous, such as 6-12-12 or 5-15-5.
- Fertilize evergreens and deciduous trees and shrubs at time of planting with 5-15-5 and with regular plant food afterwards for at least two years.

In the summer:

- Fertilize perennials after flowering.
- Do not fertilize perennials, roses, trees, shrubs, or hedges after the middle of the summer.
- Cut back annuals such as petunias and treat with a balanced fertilizer like water soluble 20-20-20 (one of my favourite maintenance fertilizers).

In the fall:

- Fertilize bulbs with superphosphate at time of planting and after flowering.

37

- Early in fall use an all-purpose fertilizer on the lawn. In late fall, an application of slow-release fertilizer will get the lawn off to a good start in the spring. This is the most important fertilizer application for your lawn in the whole year. Using slow-release fertilizers means you don't have to fertilize as frequently as they release their nutrients over months and, in some cases, years.

Don't forget to water in all dry fertilizers whenever you apply them.

CONDITIONING THE SOIL

There's one more aspect to caring for the soil. Fertilizing is all well and good, but as you might have gathered from the previous chapter and to references I've made in this one, conditioning the soil is every bit as important as fertilizing. In fact, conditioning the soil is more important than fertilizing.

Conditioning, or amending, the soil involves adding bulky matter, usually compost, to the soil. Nutrients, no matter how they are added, will not easily be released for the plants' use without a soil rich in organic matter. A soil in good condition

- will hold moisture well, but will not be water-logged;
- provides a friendly habitat for earthworms and micro-organisms that in turn continue to improve the tilth of the soil;
- allows roots to find their way easily to nutrients and grow deep in the soil where they won't quickly dry out; and

- is not compacted, which ensures that there
  will always be air available to the roots.

In my view, there are two important words when we talk of soil conditioning. One is humus; the other is mulch. I introduced you to humus in the first chapter when I was discussing composting. Humus, as you will recall, is the result of composting. It is a dark, crumbly material, with little odour which may still contain partially broken-down matter. Not only is it rich in nutrients and organic material that will feed the micro-organisms in the soil, but it can hold up to 90% of its weight in water.

USING HUMUS

Gardeners dedicated to composting feel that same rush of excitement when they "harvest" each batch of compost as they do when they see their first seedlings come up. Of course, those seedlings will be good and healthy if the seeds have been planted in humus-rich soil. Humus comes not only from compost, but from well-rotted manure, from piles of leaves left to rot, and other decomposed organic matter such as seaweed.

Humus tends to be fairly well-balanced, so you don't usually have to worry about the pH level. If the humus has been produced from a single material, such as oak leaves, it will not be as balanced as compost made from a mixture of materials. Over time — for two or more years, it's true — applications of well-rotted compost can even bring an acid or alkaline soil into balance. It supplies about six times the nutrients that an average vegetable crop requires, so if you have been digging in compost for several years, you are unlikely to need any fertilizer. If you're just starting to condition your soil with humus, you might want to continue using commercial fertilizers for a few years if your soil is poor.

Even if humus had no nutritive value, it would still be valuable in the garden because of its ability to add organic material to sandy soil and to help loosen clay. When you see your neighbours putting bags of leaves and grass clippings out for garbage pickup, you're looking at a valuable source of humus being thrown away. Make a deal with your neighbours — if they don't know about composting and don't want to know, offer to do them a favour by getting rid of their garden wastes for them. Your garden — and all the subterranean creatures that inhabit its soil — will definitely thank you.

Mulched bed   *Bare soil*

How Mulch Works

The mulched bed (left) prevents sunlight from reaching the soil, minimizing evaporation. As organic mulch decomposes it releases nutrients to the soil. In bare soil (right) heat accumulates in the soil causing evaporation and moisture stress to plants.

RULE OF THUMB:

The most important contribution you can make to your garden's overall success is the annual addition of compost, rotting leaves, and other organic material to the soil.

OTHER CONDITIONING MATERIALS

One of the great advantages of using humus as a soil conditioner is that it has already undergone decomposition, an activity that requires nitrogen. If fresh or partially decomposed material is dug into soil, you should add extra nitrogen to make up for the nitrogen the micro-organisms use to help them as they digest the organic matter.

I've taken you through the steps of making compost so that you always will have a source of this wonderful soil conditioner. Here are some more conditioners, all of which can be used in the compost pile as well.

❋ ....

MANURES: Fresh manure should never be used directly on the garden. Either add it to the compost or keep it in a pile on its own. Fresh manure can contain weed seeds, which is another reason to compost it. Chicken manure is strong, so use it with caution. use manure from vegetarian animals only as the manure from meat-eating animals may contain heavy metals.

❋ ....

WOOD BY-PRODUCTS: You can buy products such as ground bark or sawdust, or get friendly with a wood worker. Sawdust especially will deplete the soil of nitrogen as it decomposes, so if you want to dig it in, add some nitrogen (grass clippings are effective!). Don't use sawdust from pressure-treated lumber or any wood that's been treated with a preservative or paint.

LAWN CLIPPINGS: Small amounts of nitrogen-rich fresh lawn clippings can be dug directly into the garden, but large amounts should be composted first. A pile of lawn clippings on its own can build up a tremendous heat in a short time — and produce a strong, unpleasant smell! It's better to compost lawn clippings with other matter.

LEAF MOULD: You can make your own leaf mould — the remains of decomposed leaves — or buy it. To make your own, just make a compost pile that contains only leaves. You can also put leaves in plastic bags, add a bit of soil or high nitrogen fertilizer and a bit of water, leave it over the winter, and in the spring, you'll have leaf mould. Leaves from some types of trees take longer than one winter to break down, but if you do it every year, you'll have a new supply each spring.

PEAT MOSS: Peat moss, available at garden centres, is a partially decomposed organic material which is dried and packed in bales. It contains few nutrients, which it releases slowly, so it is definitely not a fertilizer. However, it can do wonders for your soil. It is somewhat acidic and is very water retentive (after all, it started its life in a bog). If it is dry when you are ready to use it, dampen it before incorporating it into the soil. Once it is dry, it can be difficult to moisten. So, if you want peat moss to increase the moisture retention of your soil, add water and stir it around. Depending on the amount and type of peat moss you have, it could take a day or two to absorb the water. By the way, this is a great Canadian product!

AERATION

I'd like briefly to mention aeration as one other way of incorporating air into soil. It is especially useful in areas that get heavy traffic, such as grass paths. Aerating is done by inserting a special tool that is hollowed out — like a large, stiff drinking straw — into the soil. Small plugs of earth are extracted that can be added to the compost pile. If you desire, you can top dress with well-rotted compost or top soil, raking it so that it falls down into the created holes. The purpose is to allow air and water to make their way to roots in compacted soil. A power aerator can be obtained from a local rent-all retailer. Split the cost with a couple of neighbours!

MULCHING

To me, mulching is a soil conditioner, although this wonderful gardening practice could just as easily be dealt with in a section on weeding or watering.

When you condition soil, you incorporate materials in to the soil. In mulching, you apply certain materials on to the bare surface of the soil in order to

- provide nutrients
- discourage weeds

- protect plants in winter
- reduce erosion
- preserve moisture
- moderate soil temperatures.

Materials for mulching are varied but some are not appropriate for all situations. Here are some good choices:

- Well-rotted compost or other humus
- Pine needles or partially rotted leaves (called leaf mould)
- Straw (try to avoid hay, which contains weed seeds)
- Seaweed
- Cocoa bean hulls
- Peat moss. It should be dampened first and is more useful when mixed with other materials as it can form a hard crust that is impervious to water
- Bark pieces (not large chips)
- Newspapers
- Pebbles or crushed stone
- Old blankets or carpets
- Plastic sheets
- Landscape fabric (polyester spun material)

MULCHING GUIDELINES Some people mulch all the time, others only at certain times of the year and under certain conditions. The following information will help you choose when and where you mulch, and decide on the materials to use in specific situations.

❊ ....

How long do you want the mulch to last? Most mulches, except the inorganic ones such as plastic, will eventually decompose, adding to the organic content of your soil. If you've got lots of mulching materials available, this may not be a problem. If your intent is also to improve the condition of the soil, you'll want an organic mulch. Some of the organic mulches can break down quickly and may need renewing several times over a gardening season.

Some of the lightweight materials may blow away. Newspapers are especially difficult in windy areas, and not particularly attractive. That is why I use them in the veggie garden. Weight them with bricks or stones, or supplement them with compost or a heavier mulch over top. If you're short of mulching material, newspapers, 6 to 8 pages thick, can make a good base over which to spread other materials.

As with soil conditioners, avoid using any material that contains poisons or anything toxic. If in doubt, don't use it.

A mulch should not go too high up the stem or trunk of a plant as it can cause rot.

Spread a layer of mulch to about 7.5 cm (3 inches) deep. Coarser materials such as loose straw will need to be deeper, about 15 cm (6 inches). Finer materials can be shallower, about 2.5 cm to 5 cm (1 to 2 inches) deep. A note of caution: Making the layers too deep can prevent water and oxygen from reaching the roots. Even if some weeds do make their way up

Here, mulch is being used to create a border between the grass and the stone retaining wall. This makes grass trimming unnecessary.

through the mulch, they're usually very easy to pull out, since they're in a weakened state.

WHEN TO MULCH Mulch has a moderating effect on the soil. A layer of mulch can prevent the soil from quickly warming up in the spring — the opposite of what you want at this time of year when the danger of frost is past. If you've mulched the previous winter, just pull the mulch away from the plants when spring comes. If you want to replace it entirely, you can add the mulch to the compost pile. If you have used large bark chips, which can take several years to break down, put them aside to be reused when the soil has warmed.

Mulch is particularly beneficial in protecting plants from the stresses of the freezing and thawing cycles that afflict us throughout the winter. This repeated freezing and thawing can have a devastating effect on plants, to the point of heaving them, roots and all, out of the ground. Many gardeners fervently wish for good snow cover every year — snow is one of the best insulators there is — but a good layer of mulch will keep the soil cold whether there's a lot of snow or not.

RULE OF THUMB:

Mulch when the soil has warmed up, and mulch when the soil has frozen.

DISADVANTAGES OF MULCHING When you mulch, you give your plants an environment in which most of them will flourish. Unfortunately, it is also an environment that some insects, especially slugs, love. It's fairly cool, it's dark, and it's damp — a slug's idea of heaven. If they really bother you, remove the mulch. On the other hand, you will have a good idea of where the slugs are if you want to go on a hunt.

Healthy soil makes healthy plants, which in turn makes happy gardeners. In this chapter I've touched on some of the nutrients that plants need and how to ensure that they are present in your soil. In the next chapter, I'll discuss heat, light, and moisture.

GROWING CONDITIONS: HEAT, LIGHT, AND WATER

J ust as you can affect the soil in your garden, you can also affect the other essential elements to plant growth: heat, light, and water.

HEAT

We can't control the weather, but to a certain extent we can regulate how much heat our seedlings and plants receive. Plants grow within the range of temperatures best suited to their species, but we humans sometimes want to push our plants to the limit of their tolerance — it's one of the fun things about being a gardener. When you garden in Canada, you can't talk about the heat without talking about the cold.

WINTER PROTECTION

Many plants need a period of cold in order to germinate or to flower. In regions with cold winters, plants become dormant and thus are able to resist damage caused by low temperatures. Once dormancy is broken, the plant begins to lose this resistance. In some parts of the country, our winters are composed of frigid temperatures that last for a week or so, followed by a respite of balmy weather — just ask any Calgarian who's experienced a chinook!

In Chapter 2 in the section *When to Mulch*, I described the stress that freezing and thawing cycles put on plants. These cycles sometimes forces the plants out of the ground so that their roots are exposed to the harsh winds and cold of winter which ultimately results in their death. Sometimes the plants get the wrong message entirely and begin to put on new growth, which then gets "nipped in the bud" by another body blow from Jack Frost! The plant might not die, but it will enter spring in a weakened state. It is also possible that its flower buds have been killed and its growth stunted.

Mulching is one method of dealing with the freezing and thawing cycles. Placing windbreaks (hedges, permanent or temporary fences) or wrapping plants (using burlap or some other fabric — but never plastic!) can also help to protect plants from the damage caused by bitter winter winds.

Windbreaks
Windbreaks will help protect large plants from damage by winter winds.

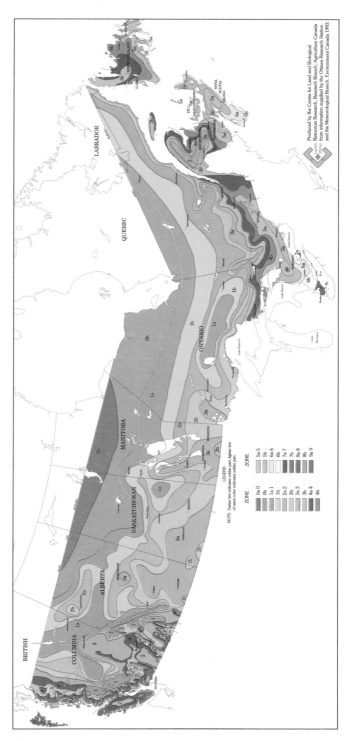

LEGEND

ZONE | ZONE
0a 0 | 5a 5
0b | 5b
1a 1 | 6a 6
1b | 6b
2a 2 | 7a 7
2b | 7b
3a 3 | 8a 8
3b | 8b
4a 4 | 9a 9
4b |

NOTE: Darker tint indicates colder part, lighter tint of same color indicates milder part.

Produced by the Centre for Land and Biological Resources Research, Research Branch, Agriculture Canada from information supplied by the Ottawa Research Station and the Meteorological Branch, Environment Canada 1993

A WORD ABOUT ZONES

Knowing the conditions each plant requires to be healthy and productive is one of the challenges of gardening. Many plant descriptions indicate the temperature ranges that are conducive to the plant's growth. These ranges are called zones and are based on a system that measures such factors as summer and winter temperatures, length of frost-free period, rainfall from spring to fall, depth of snow cover, and the strength of wind gusts. The temperature measurement is the easiest for home gardeners to understand. If you see a plant designated as hardy to Zone 5, for example, it will grow in temperatures that fall to -26°C (-15°F). The lower the zone number, the colder the winter.

Use zone designations as guidelines. Many gardeners successfully grow plants that are specified one or two zones warmer. These gardeners are taking advantage of what's known as microclimates. A microclimate can be thought of as a zone within a zone. If you live in Zone 5, for example, your garden could register as a Zone 6 for any of the following reasons:

- You live near a large body of water.
- You live on a hillside (the air will be cooler in the valley).
- Your garden faces south.
- You live in an urban area.

By using walls, fences, hedges, pathways, you can often manipulate the effect of the temperature (and thereby the zone) in your garden.

Spring Concerns

We face some of the same problems in the spring as we do in the winter. Temperatures can rise and then plummet over night. In the spring, though, there's the added complication that plants have broken their dormancy and perhaps seedlings are being set out. For most perennials, even flowering bulbs that are suddenly buried in a late spring snow, cold temperatures will not cause much damage. The rate of warming in the spring may advance or delay flowering, it's true, and may also affect the length of time the flowers stay in bloom. But the most damage can be done to tender seedlings that are being "hardened off" — put outside for longer periods to become acclimatized — or that have already been transplanted. Fortunately, there are many time-honoured methods of protecting tender plants when frost threatens or when you want to speed growth. Some methods described below also help you extend your gardening season, allowing you to get seedlings planted out early. Experiment and have fun!

Old sheets, bedspreads, dressmaker's interfacing, and curtains can be used to cover the rows of plants. Drape them over a structure so that their weight doesn't crush tender seedlings — perhaps using some sticks at either end of the row with a strong rope running the length. Commercial row covers are also available — some of them are left on even during the day, although their edges can be lifted to allow air to circulate and to prevent the build-up of high temperatures.

❃

Mini-greenhouses, called "cloches," can be fashioned from empty plastic or glass bottles and placed over individual plants. Purchased "hot caps" are available in a variety of designs and can make a big difference in the success of vegetable crops such as tomatoes.

❃

In an emergency, use overturned flowerpots, boxes, pails, or baskets as plant protectors.

❃

Cold frames — boxes with solid sides and a glass or plastic top — can be used to speed plants' growth as well as to protect them in our fickle Canadian spring weather. The top is opened on warm days but closed on cool days and at night. Closing the top traps the warmth from the soil and the air inside the box. Covering the cold frame with blankets at night will also help keep the plants warm. In the changeable spring weather, you do have to keep an eye on what's happening outside. If the temperature starts to drop or the sun disappears for hours, the top should be closed to protect the plants.

SUMMER HEAT

Some plants thrive in the hot days of summer. Others, such as lettuce, dislike the heat and will produce bitter growth and go to seed. But summer is the season of glory for most gardens. That's not to say it's without its own problems — and heat can definitely be one of them.

Hanging baskets, window boxes, and other containers dry out quickly in hot weather, especially if it is also windy. Frequent watering is necessary to keep these container plants nourished and watered. Even annuals and perennials will become stressed in hot windy weather and can quickly droop. Don't forget trees and bushes! Even though they may not show visible signs of wilting, they do need added water in summer heat. Keep mulching to conserve moisture in the soil and to prevent the soil from becoming baked.

Humid heat can give rise to mildew and other fungus problems. Good air circulation will help to prevent these diseases. Spraying with a fungicide, such as organic garden sulphur, will also control their spread. Lawns should be well watered and allowed to grow to at least 7.5 cm (3 inches) and cut no lower than 5 cm (2 inches).

RULE OF THUMB:

The longer the grass blades, the deeper the roots.

FALL PREPARATION

Many of the methods used to protect plants in the spring can be used in the fall garden to extend the season and increase the productivity of your plants. The warm days and cool evenings of fall can lull us into a false sense of security, but cold days are ahead and you have to plan for winter. Plants such as roses must have soil mounded around them or be wrapped in protective materials against the coming cold. Snow breaks, such as sections of lattice, can be constructed around evergreens to protect them from freezing winds.

WINTER PROTECTION OF ROSES

(for all Canadian growing zones except B.C.'s Lower Mainland)

Dust or spray your roses with insecticide fungicide — except your hardy shrub roses. Then, mound soil around each bush, no matter the type, to a depth of about 30 cm (12 inches). The soil can be from another part of your garden, loam, or triple mix (a mixture of compost, loam, and peat).

HYBRID TEAS, FLORIBUNDAS, GRANDIFLORAS

These roses benefit from some extra protection in addition to that afforded by mounded earth. Rose collars are used to contain insulating material such as dried leaves, shredded bark, or crumpled newspapers but have no insulating value in themselves. Don't be afraid to be generous with the newspapers — they won't hurt the roses. Alternatives to rose collars are cages that you can build with garden netting or fine-mesh chicken wire.

CLIMBING AND RAMBLING ROSES

Bend the canes to the ground as much as possible without breaking them. If possible, work on a warm day as the canes will be more flexible. This method is needed only in severe climates with some varieties.

Another method of protection is to lay them on the ground and cover them with straw held in place with burlap. Alternatively, winterize as you would a tender rose, as described above in the section on hybrid teas, and cut back the winter-killed canes in the spring.

Giving advice about rose protection can often be a prickly subject! If in doubt, check with your local rose society regarding your varieties in your area.

MINIATURE ROSES

Miniatures, for all their small size and lovely delicacy, are quite hardy. Mound some earth around them, but don't smother them. Crumpled newspaper also makes a good protective mulch. Provide more protection by lightly covering them with small evergreen branches.

TREE ROSES

If your tree rose is growing in a container, move it into a protected area such as a garage or garden shed. However, if the temperature is likely to drop much below 4°C (40°F), you should remove the plant from the container and treat it like a garden-planted rose.

If the tree rose is growing in the garden, you will need to prepare a trench for it. Dig a trench that is as long as the tree is high and deep enough so that the tree can be entirely covered with soil. Since it will be hidden from sight, be sure to mark its resting place so you don't mistakenly dig there in the early spring. The first time I tried this method, it struck me as amusing that only gardeners would dig a grave to keep something alive! You can also cover it with straw and burlap as described for climbing and rambling roses.

Tree rose (left) can be protected by bending it gently and covering it with soil and boughs (right).

LIGHT

It's easy to see how important the sun is to plants. Watch how flower heads follow the sun's progress during the day. Note how plants lean toward its rays. What is it that germinating seeds struggle towards — even those that need a period of darkness? Light!

Light makes photosynthesis happen. Photosynthesis, the most important chemical reaction in the world — for without it, life would not exist — is the process in which plants use the sun's light, in conjunction with water, to produce sugar. Without photosynthesis, plant growth would not occur.

Even plants designated as "prefers shade" or "does best on north-facing wall" need light — they just need less of it. No matter whether your garden is sunny or shady or, like most, a mixture of both, knowing about light and the various ways it is described can help you to make wise choices for your garden.

TYPES OF LIGHT

People who write about the light requirements of plants describe them in a variety of ways. Let's try to untangle what some of these terms mean.

✳ ....

SUN: Full sun all day is required for the plant to grow to the full extent of its capabilities. Most vegetables, trees, and flowers require full sun.

✳ ....

PARTIAL SHADE: Sometimes described as light shade or filtered light, this is the most ambiguous designation. It can mean anything from shade

Astilbe is a lovely perennial flower that grows in partial shade.

from a tree, which also provides some light, to sun in the morning and full shade in the afternoon. As you plan and plant your garden with partial-shade plants, ask questions and do some research to find out about your plants. For example, columbines and astilbes will grow in five to six hours of direct light or a full day of filtered light.

❁ ....

Shade: This is the shade found under a tree where no light penetrates or on the shady side of a building or wall. I equate this with the designation "deep shade."

EXPOSURE

Exposure refers to the amount of light your site receives and its duration. We also describe a garden's

Exposure

Consider how shade "travels" during the course of the day. In the left diagram the front of the house is shaded. As the sun moves, illutrated on the right, the areas of shade change so that later in the day, the front of the house is in sun.

exposure as south- or north-facing. All these terms are concerned with the same thing: what direction is the light coming from and how long will it last?

WATER

Water is another essential for growth. Even plants that have adapted to quite arid conditions rely on a period of rainfall. Most of the plants Canadian gardeners grow need supplemental watering. The water we use in our homes and gardens has undergone a lengthy and costly process of treatment to make it fit for household use. A good old-fashioned rain barrel is a wonderful way to collect water for the garden. But, no matter where the water you use comes from, use it only when the plants need a drink. Don't find yourself watering on a rigid schedule or by force of habit. Apply water according to your plants' requirements.

RULE OF THUMB:

Apply water to plants *generously* when they are in a growth mode or stage of flowering. Only allow the soil to become dry to the touch. When plants are not growing or flowering, apply water sparingly — allowing the soil to become dry about 1 cm (1/2 inch) or more below the surface.

WATERING GUIDELINES

Rules are made to be broken, and this is especially true in gardening, so I'm calling these guidelines. For each of the guidelines below, I am sure you can find someone who has done the opposite and still has a lovely garden! However, if you are having problems in your garden, review your watering techniques and follow these guidelines to see if the situation improves:

❈

Don't wait until your plants begin to droop before you water. As an indicator of need for water, stick your finger a few centimetres (a

By mounding soil into a basin around the plant, water will soak into the rootball instead of running-off.

couple of inches) into the soil. If the soil feels dry, your garden needs water.

Water plants early in the morning so that they can dry out before dark to reduce the incidence of disease. However, if the weather has been very dry, you can water in the early evening to lessen evaporation.

If possible, apply water so that it doesn't fall on leaves to avoid encouraging mildew.

Water deeply, slowly, and infrequently. One long watering is more beneficial than several short ones. Watering slowly gives the water time to seep into the soil. This is especially important for clay soils that do not absorb water quickly. Deep watering encourages roots to grow further into the soil, where they are protected from the heat of the sun and have better access to nutrients and moisture. Root vegetables such as carrots and beets benefit from deep watering.

Most herbs can withstand fairly dry conditions. Water only when leaves are drooping.

Water more frequently in hot windy weather, as this type of weather causes the plants and soil to dry out quickly.

Water annuals more frequently than perennials. Without a regular supply of water, the flowers can drop prematurely.

A hanging basket can need daily watering in the summer. Polymer crystals can be added to the soil to save water and reduce watering frequency.

❀ Water container-grown plants more frequently than garden plants.

Garden Care During Drought

Drought is often not a problem on the Canadian coasts, but in the last few years things have changed. This may be due to global warming and the greenhouse effect. So no matter where you live, be prepared for drought conditions that cause municipalities to institute watering restrictions. Here are some tips to help you garden successfully in the event of a water shortage:

❀ Apply mulch when possible to save watering. However, mulching is not appropriate for new seedlings.

❀ Add water-saving polymer crystals to garden soil or to potting soil of containers. When you water, the crystals will absorb the water, releasing it as it is needed. Some crystals should not be used on food crops.

❀ ....

Dig in organic matter to add moisture-retentive materials to the soil.

❀ ....

If you're running water in the house, don't let any run away down the drain. For example, the cold water that runs while you are waiting for the hot water to come through the pipes, or water you have used for washing dishes (this is known as grey water). Collect it and put it in rain barrels, large plastic garbage cans, or other containers to use later for watering plants in hanging baskets, window boxes, and large pots. Letting it sit awhile allows various chemicals to evaporate.

Just like you might have seen at your grandparents': A good old-fashioned rain barrel is still an excellent way to save water for use in the garden.

Soil, soil amendments, heat, light, and water — these are the elements that the gardener uses to create a garden of beauty, full of healthy plants that produce large attractive blooms and tasty, appealing fruits and vegetables. Now it's time to learn about some techniques that will keep these plants in fine form.

TECHNIQUES OF GARDENING

· ·

Maintenance of your garden, after soil preparation, is the key to success. In our busy lives, the garden gives us respite from the daily hurly-burly, so the maintenance techniques you use should not be onerous or time-consuming. Taking time to smell the roses is more important than taking time to prune them!

CULTIVATING

Cultivating can be used to mean any of the following:

- breaking up the soil
- tilling or working the ground with a tool, implement, or machine
- tending or nurturing plants

BREAKING UP THE SOIL

To prepare new beds, it is usually necessary to dig, although there are some methods that don't involve digging, but they take longer to prepare the soil for planting. A tiller will have difficulty breaking through grass, so digging remains the best alternative for breaking up soil in an existing lawn. Here are some guidelines for preparing new beds:

❋ Fall is a good time to prepare new beds.

❋ One method is to turn the turf over, leaving large clumps of soil. In the spring, much of the grass and other plant material in the clods will have broken down. Break up the clods, taking out large pieces of plant material that haven't decomposed.

❋ Another method is to pile leaves or mulching materials over the chosen area. Leave over the winter or even over the summer, adding more materials as needed. The idea is to stop the growth of the existing plants, usually grass. By using mulching materials, you are also enriching the soil. It's true that while you're waiting for the grass to die, the pile might not be very attractive, but after a few months, you will be able easily to dig in the mulching material and start planting. Black plastic sheets can also be used in the same way.

❋ The soil you are digging should not be wet. Digging can compact the particles and destroy the structure of the soil. Dig a test shovelful — if it falls apart easily, it is ready for digging. If it doesn't fall apart easily, wait a few days and test again.

❋ Remove existing grass to make digging easier. Use a lawn edger or sharp spade to cut through and under the grass. Roll the sod up and use it to patch worn areas of the lawn. You could also turn it

upside down in the compost pile or bury it upside
down in the new bed, where it will decompose.

❀ ....

Remove any weeds, taking care to get their roots.

❀ ....

Dig well-rotted compost or manure into the
bed using a fork or spade.

Roto Tilling

Tilling is a technique used usually in vegetable
gardens, especially when the plants are still young.
By using a rotary tiller between the rows, you can
quickly mix soil amendments and fertilizers into
the top 15 cm (6 inches) of soil at the same as you
turn under weeds. The action also helps to incorporate air into the soil.

Tending

The word cultivate is also used to describe the general process of tending to plants, especially weeding
with a tool such as a hoe or small fork. This has the
same advantages as tilling — mixing air into the soil,
loosening compacted soil, and getting rid of weeds.

RAKING

We all associate rakes with autumn leaves, but
rakes are used for other garden tasks. Choose the
appropriate rake for the job.

Fan rakes (soft rakes) with light tines, such as
bamboo or plastic, are good for

- raking leaves
- dislodging thatch from the lawn (never use a
  hard rake on a lawn)

Metal-headed rakes (hard rakes) are better for
- smoothing and levelling soil
- gathering debris from around plants
- covering over freshly planted seeds
- working materials into the surface of the soil
- distributing mulch evenly

STAKING

Many plants, such as newly planted trees or heavy-headed flowering plants, need some kind of support.

STAKING TREES

Newly planted trees often need staking until their roots can support them. The stakes should be left in place no longer than two years; that should be sufficient time for the roots to become established and the trunk strong enough to withstand high winds.

Two or three stakes evenly-spaced around a tree provide better support than a single stake.

✿

Although it is possible to use only one stake, two or three spaced evenly around the tree are better.

✿

The ties that connect the stakes to the tree should be a of soft material, such as nylon webbing or inner-tube rubber. Avoid using wire or anything that will bite into or rub the trunk.

STAKING FLOWERING PLANTS

Tall flowering plants such as delphiniums, hollyhocks, and gladiolus often need staking, especially if they are growing in a windy location. Floppy plants, such as asters, coreopsis, and carnations, can benefit from support, too.

✿

STAKES: Bamboo canes or sturdy stakes about 2.5 cm (1 inch) square make good solid supports. Choose stakes that will be able to support the height of the mature plant. Sharpen the bottom of the stake to make it easier to drive into the ground.

✿

TIES: Ties are needed to attach the stake to the plant. Use a material that's soft and won't damage the stem. Good choices are twine, rubber strips, bicycle tire tubing, wide elastic bands, and cloth strips. As the plant grows, tie the stem loosely to the stake. When it reaches its mature height, cut off any stake that protrudes above it.

✿

WIRE CAGES: Short plants with many stems can be supported by wire cages, similar to ones available for tomatoes. The foliage will hide the cage as the plant grows.

Staking Flowers *(left) Inserting a length of tube when planting a seedling allows a stake to easily be positioned when needed without disturbing the plant's roots. (right) Floppy plants, like sweet pea, can be supported by tree branches.*

✽ ....

WIRE HOOPS: Attach a ring of heavy wire to several stakes and insert it around the plant either when it begins to grow or at planting time. As the plant grows, slide the hoop higher.

GROWING FROM SEED

For me, gardening is a year-round activity. Even when I'm not doing it, I'm thinking about it. When the many great Canadian seed catalogues start arriving on snowy winter days, I know I'll soon be able to turn from the thinking and dreaming to doing some indoor gardening. A list of some Canadian seed sources will be found on page 90.

Starting plants from seeds is a rewarding aspect of gardening. It's not hard to do and you don't need a lot of fancy equipment. As you become more confident, you can move from easy germinators, such as tomatoes, cosmos, dianthus, petunias, and pansies, to trickier ones, such as poppies, lavender, and impatiens.

ADVANTAGES OF GROWING FROM SEED

The advantages of growing from seed outweigh the disadvantages — in fact, it's hard to think of what the disadvantages could be. Although, if you take over every windowsill and other surface near a window, family members might object!

❀ You can have dozens of plants for the price of a few seedlings bought at a garden centre.

❀ You know the conditions the plants were grown under, since you provide the growing medium and all nutrients.

❀ A wider range of colours and varieties is available by seed than in garden centre seedlings.

❀ You will have a great feeling of enjoyment and satisfaction as you watch your seedlings grow, and it is a wonderful way to get kids interested in gardening.

SEEDLING EXCHANGE

Set up a seedling exchange with your gardening friends. Each of you can specialize in one particular plant, then trade with one another when the seedlings are ready to be transplanted. If, for example, your green thumb is successful with nasturtiums, sow enough for both you and your friends. If someone else is successful with lamb's ears and yours have been a dud, you have a ready-made barter.

GETTING STARTED

Seeds need warmth and moisture to germinate. Some seeds need dark conditions, others need bright light. Some need to be kept in the cold for a period of time (called *stratification*), others need their hard seed coatings nicked (called *scarification*). If you are a beginner, it's best to stay away from some of these demanding seeds until you have had success with easier seeds. Seed packets usually give you all the detail you need.

Here's what you need to get started:

❊ ....

A growing medium. A purchased soilless mix is the ideal medium in which to start seeds. Most mixes are a combination of peat moss, vermiculite, perlite, and often added nutrients.

❊ ....

Small containers. Some means of enclosing the containers to conserve moisture is important, too, because until the seeds germinate, they'll need to be kept in a warm, damp atmosphere. A shallow tray with drainage makes a good container, but there are many other possibilities: purchased peat pots or plastic pots; margarine tubs; sour cream, cottage cheese, or yogurt containers; the bottom half of milk cartons or plastic bottles; tin cans; old muffin tins; styrofoam or paper cups. All containers should be very clean to avoid introducing diseases. **Make drainage holes in those containers that don't have any.**

❊ ....

A light source. A south- or west-facing window is ideal. An overhead fluorescent light can produce

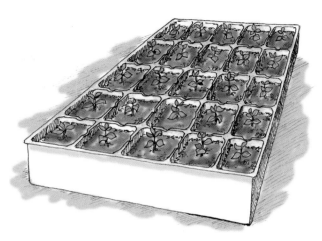

A seed tray should contain a purchased soilless mix as the growing medium.

excellent results as well. It should be mounted about 10 cm to 12.5 cm (4 to 5 inches) from the top of the seedlings. There's no need to spend a lot of money — it's easy to rig up a light stand using some plumbing piping or left-over lumber. The light can also be hung from the ceiling.

PLANTING THE SEEDS

Fill the pot or flat with the soilless mix and smooth the surface. Sow the seeds in rows if using a flat or scatter the seeds on top of the mix in a pot. If the seed packet doesn't specify spacing, plant the seeds about a finger's width apart.

Cover the seeds with a thin layer of the mix or finely ground up vermiculite. Water carefully with a fine mist. Water every day or as the surface dries, and cover to hold the moisture until germination.

Mark the seedlings with a plastic or wooden label; write the names with a pencil or pen with waterproof ink.

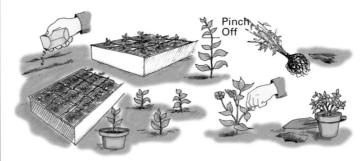

Pinch Off

Growing Annuals

Sow seeds (left) in a seed box and as they grow move them in to progressively larger containers. After hardening off (centre), the seedlings are transplanted to the garden. Pinching off lanky growth encourages bushier plants (right top). Pull up and destroy annuals in the fall or (right lower) cut plants back, pot them and bring indoors.

Cover the container with a plastic bag, glass, or some type of see-through covering. Depending on the requirements of your seeds, put them in a warm dark place or in the light. The seed packet will give directions. If it doesn't, assume that the seed should be covered before germination.

As soon as the seeds have germinated — that is, when you see the first green shoot — remove the cover and expose to as much light as possible.

DAMPING OFF

The main problem you are likely to encounter is a condition called *damping off* — the plants suddenly wilt and collapse. Damping off is a fungus disease that arises as a result of the conditions the seeds and seedlings need: warmth and moisture. Water the plants with a fungicide specially formulated for this purpose, called "No Damp," available at most garden centres.

TRANSPLANTING

When the seedlings have developed several sets of leaves or when the container is getting crowded, they should be transplanted.

❀

Prepare another set of containers, enough to take a seedling in each one. Fill them with potting soil.

❀

Gently take the seedling from the pot, holding it by its leaves (never by its stem) and using a pencil to help loosen it. Use the pencil to tease the soilless mix from the seedling's roots.

❀

Poke a hole into the potting soil in the new container and lower the seedling into it, placing it at the same depth that it grew in the first pot. Firm the soil around the roots, again using the pencil.

Continue to provide water, light, and warmth. Now that the seedlings have been transplanted, a half-strength solution of 10-52-10 fertilizer can be administered every week. Light is one of the most important conditions. Seedlings can grow leggy — their stems and leaves become weak and floppy as they stretch to the light source. If your light source is a window, turn the plants at least once a day so they will grow straight.

HARDENING OFF

As spring days begin to warm up, your seedlings should be set outside for short periods of time. This process, called *hardening off*, exposes them to the elements: sun, wind, and rain. However, in the beginning, too much of any one could cause their

Correct Planting in Pots
Cover the drainage hole with bits of broken pots, be sure the pot is the right size for the root mass and allow adequate space between the soil level and the top of the pot to hold water until it seeps in.

demise. The first few times you put them out, shelter them from direct sun and winds, and don't put them out in a pelting rain. As they strengthen, leave them out for longer periods but keep an eye on them. Because they're in small pots, they can dry out quickly.

Eventually, your seedlings will be able to be left out all night. If you have a cold frame, they can spend nights in it. If you haven't got a cold frame, either bring them indoors when frost threatens or protect them in one of the ways I described in Chapter 3 under *Protecting Seedlings*.

When all danger of frost has passed, plant the seedlings in your garden.

PROPAGATION

Growing by seed is not the only method of propagating your own plants. You can increase your plant stock by taking cuttings and dividing plants.

Taking Cuttings

Tip Cuttings: House plants, tender perennials, and annuals (especially geraniums) are often propagated from cuttings of soft new growth of tips that haven't flowered. Don't take cuttings from plants about to bloom or which are blooming profusely.

❊ ⋯⋯⋯⋯⋯⋯⋯⋯⋯⋯⋯⋯⋯⋯⋯⋯⋯

Prepare the potting soil, half peat and half clean sharp sand. Moisten it well and fill the pots with it.

❊ ⋯⋯⋯⋯⋯⋯⋯⋯⋯⋯⋯⋯⋯⋯⋯⋯⋯

Take cuttings about 10 cm (4 inches) long, making the cut slightly below the node — the little bump on a stem from which a leaf or root will grow. Remove leaves from the bottom half of the cutting and apply a rooting hormone to the bottom cut. Insert the cutting into the soil to no more than 2.5 cm (1 inch), but so that at least one node is below the surface. Don't let leaves touch the soil or each other.

❊ ⋯⋯⋯⋯⋯⋯⋯⋯⋯⋯⋯⋯⋯⋯⋯⋯⋯

Water the cuttings well and keep them moist. Put the pot in a plastic bag. In order to avoid

Protecting Cuttings
The clear plastic bag is supported by a wire frame to keep it clear of the cuttings.

diseases, don't let the covering touch the cuttings. Another option is to cover them with a plastic hood or put them in an unused aquarium covered with glass or plastic. Open the covering once a day to allow for air circulation. Place in indirect light.

Most cuttings will root in seven to ten days. Once you're sure they are rooted, gradually give them more ventilation and sun. When the cuttings are growing, you can fertilize them every two weeks. Give them winter protection in their first year.

Root Cuttings: This method is used most often for berries, as well as ornamentals with fleshy roots such as bleeding heart, Oriental poppy, lily, and peony.

❀

Carefully dig up the plant and wash the soil off the roots in the late summer, fall, or early spring when it is dormant. Choose roots that are vigorous and fairly thick. With a clean sharp knife sterilized in alcohol, cut the roots off close to the crown of the parent. Replant the parent immediately.

❀

Cut the roots into 5 cm to 10 cm (2 to 4 inch) pieces. Cut the bottom end at a slant. Before planting the cuttings, dip them in a solution of one part bleach to twenty parts water to sterilize them. Insert the pieces, slanted end first, in pots or flats filled with a mixture of half peat moss and half sand or perlite. Cover the tops with 6 mm (1/4 inch) of this mixture.

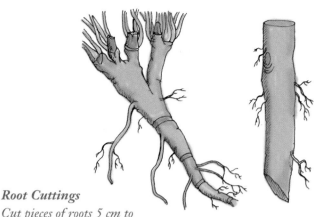

Root Cuttings
*Cut pieces of roots 5 cm to
10 cm (2 to 4 inches) long with
square tops and a tapering base.*

❋

Cover the container with a plastic bag or piece
of glass. Keep the cuttings just barely moist —
wet soil will cause them to rot. Put the pots or
flats in a cold frame, a bright unheated room, or
under artificial lights; if possible, provide bottom heat. When two or three sets of leaves
appear, plant the cuttings in individual pots,
which can also be kept in a cold frame and over
the winter, if necessary.

DIVIDING PERENNIALS

Spring and fall are the best times to divide perennials, but some plants are better divided at particular times of the year. Here are some tips to help
you plan your dividing.

❋

Generally, divide perennials that bloom in the
summer or fall in the spring. Divide spring-
blooming perennials in the late spring or early
summer, after they have bloomed.

Dividing Perennials
Take a clump of roots from the outside growth area and divide it with two garden forks or spades.

❋

The very best conditions for dividing, whether spring or fall, are overcast days.

❋

Two of the benefits of dividing in the fall are the autumn rains and the cool evening temperatures that will help your new plants get established. If there is a period of drought, however, water a couple of times a day, especially if the weather is windy.

❋

In the spring, divide perennials when new growth is just visible.

PLANTING THE NEW DIVISION

Some plants are so easy to divide that not much digging is necessary. Plants such as coreopsis and chrysanthemums are in this group. They tend to have shallow matted roots that can easily be torn apart by hand and transplanted. However, plants with deeper or matted roots need to be dug out of their beds.

❄ Thoroughly water the clump of plants you are going to divide.

❄ Prepare the new planting hole for the divisions. Enrich the soil with compost or well-rotted manure.

❄ Cut stalks back to 5 cm to 8 cm (2 to 3 inches).

❄ Use a sharp spade to dig a clump of the plant. The size will depend on what you can easily lift. Dig several clumps if you want to spare your back! The best sections for transplanting are usually the sections on the outside of the old clump — this is where the new growth is taking place. The centre of the old plant is not worth replanting.

❄ Divide the clump into the sizes you want, but be sure to keep good strong roots in each section. You can either tear the clumps apart, or use your shovel or a sharp knife to cut tougher root masses. If the roots are tightly intertwined, take two garden forks and insert them back to back through the centre of the root mass. Push them apart to separate the sections — you might have to wiggle them back and forth several times if the root is very woody and matted.

❄ Place the new clump in the prepared hole to the same depth it was planted before.

❄ Use 5-15-5 transplanter fertilizer and water well. It is a good idea to mulch, especially if you are doing your dividing late in the fall.

❁ Protect the roots if you are not able to plant the new division immediately. Cover them with a damp cloth, such as burlap, or plunge the plant into a pail of water. Other options are to "heel" the plant in — that is, lay the plant on top of the bed and cover the roots with soil — or to plant it temporarily in a container or pot. These latter two methods are particularly good if you need to wait several days or even weeks before you replant the divisions.

❁ Fertilize the following spring, April through July, with a 6-12-12 fertilizer.

PRUNING

One of the simplest acts of pruning is dead-heading. It is easy because you know exactly when to do it — when the flower head is dead just cut it off! It is that simple. The reward is many more beautiful blooms. What are the purposes of pruning? Pruning

❁ makes a plant look better and stimulates the plant to put out more growth;

❁ can increase the production of fruits, flowers, and leaves;

❁ opens the interior of a plant, improving air circulation, which helps prevent disease and insect attacks.

PRUNING TERMINOLOGY

You will come across the following terms as you learn more about pruning.

❋

Dead-heading is removing spent flowers. It increases the production of more flowers as the plant is prevented from producing seed. It then puts energy into making more flowers.

❋

Pinching removes the buds at the ends of branches and stems (called terminal buds). This term is usually used when talking about house plants and flowers.

❋

Shearing applies to hedges and other plants where a thick, dense look is desired.

❋

Thinning is a process of taking out individual branches to give a lighter, more open look.

Pruning Principle
Left: Correct pruning where the twig or branch is cut .5 cm (1/4 inch) above a bud pointing in the direction you want the branch to grow, making the cut slanting. Centre left: Not good because the cut is too long and angled Centre right: This cut is too long and, at right, the cut is too close to the bud.

PRUNING TECHNIQUES

There's nothing like pruning to put even the most experienced gardener into a dither. Where to cut brings us to a halt as we stand before the plant. Remember these few simple guidelines when you are preparing for your next pruning task.

❈ Plants grow from their buds, especially the terminal buds. Removing these buds causes new growth to come from other buds along the stem. This causes the branch to look leafier and fuller.

❈ Cut back to a bud pointing in the direction you want the new growth to go. Make the cut about 0.5 cm (1/4 inch) above the bud at an angle that has the highest part at the side of the stem that carries the bud.

❈ Cut out branches that cross or rub one another; branches that grow back into the centre of the plant; and diseased or weak branches.

***Correct Pruning of
a Shrub***
*Removing small or
weak branches will
create a stronger shrub
with better foliage.*

WHEN TO PRUNE

Generally, it's best to prune when a plant is not under stress. For example, don't prune when a plant is dry, when it's going into winter, or when it's diseased or suffering insect attacks. One of the most important things you need to know about flowering shrubs and vines is whether they bloom on old wood or new wood. Plants such as forsythia that bloom on old wood should be pruned after they have bloomed; plants such as PeeGee hydrangea and Rose of Sharon that bloom on new wood should be pruned in late winter or spring, just as growth starts.

Foliage plants can be pruned at any time except in the fall. Pruning causes the plant to put on new growth and this new growth will be too tender to survive the winter. If a mature tree or shrub needs a fairly major pruning, don't do it all at once. Spread the job over two or three years by pruning away about a third of the growth each year.

Correct Pruning of a Hedge
Hedges should be narrower at the top than the bottom.

> **RULE OF THUMB:**
> Prune hardy flowering shrubs within one month following the flowering period. Lilac, spirea, etc., all respond well to this timing.

WEEDING

I find weeding an enjoyable and relaxing garden task, providing I am pulling young weeds!. It gets me in among my plants where I can examine them up close as I pull out the invaders. Even though I enjoy it, I do try to cut down on the amount of weeding my garden needs.

We weed our gardens because weeds steal nourishment and moisture from the plants we want to grow. They provide aggressive competition for valuable resources if left unchecked. They also can detract from the beauty of the garden we have planned so carefully. Here are some handy tips to keep your garden free of weeds.

❈ Mulch. Try it — it works! (See Chapter 2 under the section on *Mulching*.)

❈ Keep weeds out of the lawn by setting the blade of your mower at 5 cm (2 inches). Don't give weed seeds a chance to find a space to grow.

❈ Plant flowerbeds densely — again, you are not giving the weeds a spot to put down their roots.

❈ Destroy not only the flower and seed heads of weeds but the roots as well when clearing ground for new beds.

❋ ....

Use the hoe as the first line of attack if weeds have taken over. It is easier than hand-pulling and will not harm other plants.

❋ ....

Use herbicides for situations that won't respond to any of the above methods. Discuss your problem with a professional at a garden centre. Make sure you understand the ramifications of using a particular type of herbicide. Great care must be taken not to kill the desired plants as well as the undesired weeds.

DISEASES AND INSECTS

In spite of all your loving attention, disaster can strike — your hostas have holes the size of loonie coins in them, the leaves on your roses have orange spots, and your cabbages look like bug condos. The first step is to identify the culprit. Some of the most common symptoms, their causes, and treatment are listed below. Other diseases and insects exist, of course, but many garden problems can be attributed to the ones given here.

DISEASES

❋ ....

Symptom: White powdery substance on upper surface of leaves
Cause: Powdery mildew, which occurs when humidity is high
Treatment: Improve air circulation; treat with fungicide.

❄ ....

Symptom: Brown water-soaked spots on petals, flowers, or leaves; buds don't open
Cause: Botrytis blight; can be severe in high humidity
Treatment: Destroy affected parts; improve draining ability of soil; treat with fungicide.

❄ ....

Symptom: Rusty orange spots on leaves and stems
Cause: Rust
Treatment: Destroy affected parts; try to keep foliage dry; treat with fungicide (Bordo spray).

❄ ....

Symptom: Black spots on rose leaves; leaves become yellow and drop
Cause: Black spot
Treatment: Clean up fallen leaves; treat with fungicide, such as garden sulphur; as prevention, use lime sulphur and dormant spray in spring. Spray soil as well as plant as this is a soil-born disease.

❄ ....

Symptom: Wilting plants, discoloured leaves
Cause: Wilt or under/over watering
Treatment: Check soil with finger for watering problem. If water is not the problem, destroy the entire plant.

INSECTS

❄ ....

Symptom: Sticky "honeydew" appears on stems and leaves; clusters of small insects at tips of stems
Cause: Aphids
Treatment: Spray with water to knock to

ground, where some will perish; spray with rotenone, pyrethrum, or insecticidal soap or Trounce (organic).

❀

Symptom: Holes in leaves
Cause: Slugs or earwigs
Treatment: Earwigs: trap in dark places by putting out newspapers, corrugated cardboard, or hoses; shake out into soapy water in morning. Slugs: sprinkle around affected plants with any of: dry wood ashes, talc, lime, diatomaceous earth, or sand. In both cases, keep garden clear of debris. Check at garden centre to review products available to deal with these pests.

❀

Symptom: Fine silky webbing on foliage
Cause: Mites
Treatment: Insect is almost invisible; spray with Trounce, concentrating on underside of leaves. Keep foliage wet as often as possible.

❀

Symptom: Seedlings suddenly topple over at soil level
Cause: Cutworm
Treatment: Protect newly planted seedlings with a paper collar or open-ended tin placed around stems; treat with insecticidal soap.

CANADIAN SEED CATALOGUES

Canadian seed and plant catalogues are available from
the following:

CATALOGUE	ADDRESS	TELEPHONE/FAX
Aimers Seeds	81 Temperance St., Aurora, ON, L4G 2R1	905-841-6226/ 905-727-7333
Alberta Nurseries & Seeds Ltd.	Box 20, Bowden, AB, T0M 0K0	403-224-3545/ 403-224-2455
Beachwood Daylily and Perennial	Box 60240 Fraser Postal Outlet, Vancouver, BC, V5W 4B5	604-874-9451
Beckers Seed Potatoes	R.R.1, Trout Creek, ON, P0H 2L0	705-724-2305
Canadian Wildflower Society	Unit 12A, Box 228, 4981 Highway 7 East, Markham, ON, L3R 1N1	905-294-9075
Corn Hill Nursery Ltd.	R.R.5, Route 890, Petitcodiac, NB, E0A 2H0	506-756-3635/ 506-756-1087
Country Lane Herbs and Dried Flowers	R.R. 3, Puslinch, ON, N0B 2J0	905-659-7327
Cruickshank's Inc.	780 Birchmount Rd., Unit 16, Scarborough, ON, M1K 5H4	416-750-9249/ 416-750-8522
William Dam Seeds	Box 8400, Dundas, ON, L9H 6M1	905-628-6641
Dominion Seed House	Box 2500, Georgetown, ON, L7G 5L6	905-873-3037 1-800-784-3037/ 1-800-567-4594

Gardenimport Inc.	Box 760, Thornhill, ON, L3T 4A5	905-731-1950
Gardens North	5984 Third Line Rod. N., R.R.3, North Gower, ON, K0A 2T0	613-489-0065/ same
Halifax Seed Co. Inc.	Box 8026, 5860 Kane St., Halifax, NS, B3K 5L8	902-454-7456
The Herb Farm	R.R.4, Norton, NB, E0G 2N0	506-839-2140
Hortico Inc.	723 Robson Rd., R.R.1, Waterdown, ON, L0R 2H1	905-689-9323/ 905-689-6566
Island Specialty Nursery	8797 Chemainus Rd., R.R.1, Chemainus, BC, V0R 1K0	604-246-9355/ 604-246-4528
Mason Hogue Gardens	3520 Durham Rd. 1 (Brock Road), R.R.4, Uxbridge, ON, L9P 1R4	
McFayden Seed Co. Ltd.	30 9th St., Suite 200, Brandon, MB, R7A 6N4	204-725-7300
Moore Water	Box 70, Dept. CG, Port Stanley, ON, N5L 1J4	519-782-4052
Mori Miniatures	Box 772, Virgil, ON, L0S 1T0	905-468-0315/ 905-468-7271
Ontario Seed Co. Ltd.	Box 7, 330 Phillip St., Waterloo, ON,N2J 3Z9	519-886-0557/ 519-886-0605
Carl Pallek & Son Nurseries	Box 137, Virgil, ON, L0S 1T0	905-468-7262
Pickering Nurseries Inc.	870 Kingston Rd., Pickering, ON, L1V 1A6	905-839-2111
Picov's Water Garden & Fisheries Centre	380 Kingston Rd., East, Ajax, ON, L1S 4S7	905-686-2151/ 905-686-2183

PLANTING & GROWING

Prairie Grown Garden Seeds	Box 118, Cochin, SK, S0M 0L0	306-386-2737
Reimer Waterscapes	Box 34, Tillsonburg, ON, N4G 4H3	519-842-6049/ 519-688-5459
Richters	357 Highway 47, Goodwood ON, L0C 1A0	905-640-6677
Stokes Seeds Ltd.	39 James St., Box 10, St. Catharines, ON, L2R 6R6	905-688-4300/ 905-684-8411
T & T Seeds Ltd.	Box 1710, Winnipeg, MB, R3C 3P6	204-956-2777/ 204-956-1994
Tregunno Seeds	126 Catharine St. N., Hamilton, ON, L8R 1J4	905-528-5984/ 905-528-1635
Vesey's Seeds Ltd.	York, Box 9000, Charlottetown, PE, C1A 8K6	902-368-7333/ 902-566-1620

❀ NOTES: ❀

....

....

....

....

....

....

....

....

....

....

....

....

....

....

....

....

....

....

INDEX

See all 4 volumes in *The Complete Gardener* series:

Simplifies the process of design and demystifies the issue of colour. Essential information for planning your garden so it looks its best. Includes planting instructions on making your own all-white garden regardless of your garden size. Accompanied by video.

⚬⚬⚬

Learn how to add interest and charm through the furnishings in your garden. From arbours to urns—they're here! Features step-by-step directions for making and planting a "stone" trough that would cost a small fortune to buy! Accompanied by video.

These fundamentals of good gardening practice will help you to create and keep a garden full of blooming, healthy plants. Don't miss the recipe for compost tea—your plants will love it! Accompanied by video.

⚬⚬⚬

Helps you select the best annuals, perennials, vines, ground covers, trees and shrubs and bulbs for your growing conditions. Special instructions on how to plant a beautiful four-season window box. Accompanied by video.